Poptropica®

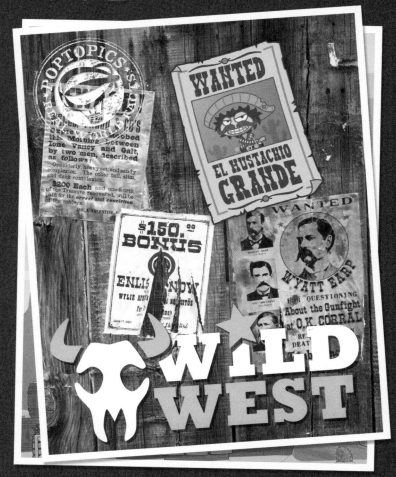

by Tracey West

Poptropica
An Imprint of Penguin Group (USA) LLC

POPTROPICA
Published by the Penguin Group
Penguin Group (USA) LLC, 375 Hudson Street, New York, New York 10014, USA

USA | Canada | UK | Ireland | Australia | New Zealand | India | South Africa | China

penguin.com
A Penguin Random House Company

The publisher does not have any control over and does not assume any responsibility for author or third-party websites or their content.

Photo credits: cover and page i: © konstantin32/iStock/Thinkstock; page 3: © Wavebreakmedia Ltd/ Wavebreak Media/Thinkstock; page 6: © Sean Hannah/iStock/Thinkstock; page 7: © Charlotte Couchman/ iStock/Thinkstock; page 13: © Comstock/Stockbyte/Thinkstock; page 19: (Appaloosa horse running) © Lenka Dankova/iStock/Thinkstock, (horse in stall) © Joel Carillet/iStock/Thinkstock; page 20: © Fuse/Fuse/ Thinkstock; page 21: (Brahman bull) © Melissa Carroll/iStock/Thinkstock, (Angus cattle) © Mark Hatfield/ iStock/Thinkstock; page 23: © duncan1890/iStockphoto; page 30: © jim pruitt/iStock/Thinkstock; page 32: © ehrlif/iStock/Thinkstock; page 33: © SandSandS/iStock/Thinkstock; page 34: Courtesy of Library of Congress, Prints & Photographs Division; page 36: (black train) © stokkete/iStock/Thinkstock, (rusty train) © Valery Kraynov/iStock/Thinkstock, (tracks) © James Feliciano/iStock/Thinkstock; page 38: © Mark Hayes/ iStock/Thinkstock; page 44: (antique camera) © Francois Lariviere/Hemera/Thinkstock, (Sullivan's photo) Courtesy of Library of Congress, Prints & Photographs Division; page 46: © stocksnapper/iStock/Thinkstock; page 48: © Vincent Giordano/Hemera/Thinkstock; page 50, 51, 52, 55, 56, 57, 58: Courtesy of Library of Congress, Prints & Photographs Division; page 60: © Troy Snow/iStock/Thinkstock; page 61: © Troy Snow/ iStock/Thinkstock; page 62: (mule) © jeanma85/iStock/Thinkstock, (beef goulash) © barol16/iStock/Thinkstock.

ISBN 978-0-448-48047-3   10 9 8 7 6 5 4 3 2 1

Connecting Poptropica to the Real World

When you enter Poptropica, you can explore different times, countries, and even planets with the stroke of a keyboard. And while you might be able to do amazing things like battle robots and defy gravity, you should know that every Island is somehow connected to the real world.

This book takes a real-world look at **Wild West Island.** There, you step into the boots of the Marshal of Dusty Gulch to defend the town from El Mustachio Grande and his Grande Gang. Dusty Gulch is based on a typical town in the American Old West, and so are the Poptropicans you'll meet there.

So what are you waiting for? Hop in the saddle and get ready for a wild ride to the Old West!

In this book, you'll read some words and phrases used by cowboys in the Old West. Look for this symbol to help decipher this cowboy slang.

GO WEST!

These days, there are few areas of the world that we can't glimpse by clicking a button on a keyboard. Forests,

mountains, oceans, deserts—they've all been explored, photographed, and posted on the Web.

But not too long ago, most people didn't know what most of the United States looked like. It's a pretty big place—the forty-eight states (and Washington, DC) that make up the contiguous United States have an area of more than three million miles. That's a lot of land, and until the 1800s, most of it had yet to be explored by the Europeans who had settled on the coasts.

The promise of new landscapes, new animals, and encounters with new people spurred many adventurous spirits to make their way out west.

HOW THE WEST WAS SETTLED

Take a look at a map of the United States, and you'll see why the West and East Coasts were the first to be settled by Europeans. In the 1600s, the English and Dutch sailed the Atlantic to settle the East. In the 1700s, Spanish missionaries sailed up the West Coast from Mexico to colonize what we know today as California. So what about those thousands of miles in between? Take a trip through time on these pages to find out what led to the development of the wild frontier.

More Land: In 1803, President Thomas Jefferson doubled the size of the United States with the Louisiana Purchase. He paid $15 million for all the land between the Mississippi River and the Rocky Mountains, and from Canada to New Orleans.

Explorers Set Out: In 1804, Meriwether Lewis and William Clark set out on a two-year expedition to explore the uncharted territory between Missouri and the Pacific Ocean.

Freedom for Mexico: After a long revolution, Mexico became independent from Spain in 1821 and took control of New Mexico and Texas.

Faster Travel: In 1807, Robert Fulton and Robert Livingston made news by demonstrating a steamboat that cut down the time of river travel by more than half.

Pushing West: The Erie Canal was finished in 1825, making it easier for East Coasters to get to the Great Lakes in the northwest US.

Tragic History: President Andrew Jackson pushed for the Indian Removal Act. It was passed in 1830 and gave him the right to remove American Indians from their land east of the Mississippi and force them into the West.

Cattle Ranches: In the 1850s, Americans developed a taste for beef. The cattle-ranching industry started to grow, and the vast plains of the frontier were perfect for grazing cattle.

Free Land!: The US government passed the Homestead Act in 1862, giving free land to farmers in exchange for their care of the land. Pioneers flocked to the West for a chance to start a new life.

Gold Rush: After gold was discovered in California in 1848 thousands of fortune hunters traveled across the country, establishing towns and cities. Two years later, California became a state.

Even Faster Travel: The First Transcontinental Railroad was ready to roll in 1869, shortening the trip west (previously six to eight months) to only one week.

End of an Era: By the end of the nineteenth century, westward expansion had slowed. One reason: the invention of barbed wire in 1874. Ranchers could now keep their cattle contained, and they no longer needed cowboys to herd them as they wandered across the prairie.

A Nation at War: Still occupied by Mexico, Texas was made a state in 1845. By 1846, Mexico and the United States were at war. The war ended in 1848, and the United States came away with new territory, which included what we now know as Arizona, New Mexico, Nevada, Texas, Utah, and western Colorado.

Blazing a Trail: In the 1840s, the Oregon Trail cleared the way for a two-thousand-mile journey from Missouri to Oregon. Hundreds of thousands of people used the trail to travel west.

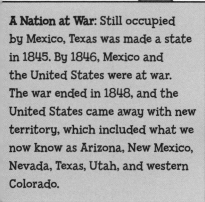

More Tragedy: In 1838, sixteen thousand Cherokee Indians were forcibly made to move west. Between two thousand and four thousand of them died on the long march, which became known as the Trail of Tears.

Texas Rebels: Fighting broke out between Texas and Mexico in 1836, after Texas leaders declared independence.

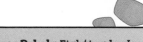

THE GREAT PLAINS

In Wild West Island, you'll ride your horse across the plains—part of the larger area known as the Great Plains. How can something be *great* and *plain* at the same time? Well, *plain* is a geographical term for a large, flat area without a lot of trees. And the *great* refers to the size of the Great Plains region in the United States—it's an area of more than a million square miles, which is about one-third the size of the United States. This vast stretch of land is where the stage was set for the Wild West.

The Plain Facts:

- Not all scientists agree on the boundaries of the Great Plains.
- From south to north, the Great Plains roughly stretch from the Rio Grande up into lower Canada.
- From west to east, the region roughly stretches from the Rocky Mountains to the eastern borders of North Dakota, South Dakota, Nebraska, Kansas, Oklahoma, and Texas.
- The Great Plains aren't all flat. They contain many hills, valleys, and streams.
- Today, crops such as wheat, corn, and cotton are grown on the Great Plains.

One Big Salad Bar

Back in the 1800s, much of the Great Plains were covered with grasses. Millions of wild buffalo grazed on this land, and cattle ranchers discovered it was perfect for raising herds of cattle.

Dinosaur fossils have been found in rocks on the western part of the Great Plains. The fossils date back to the Cretaceous period (about sixty-five million years ago).

Wild West Animals

A cowboy riding on the Great Plains might encounter prairie dogs, coyotes, prairie chickens, and deadly rattlesnakes along the trail. Hidden in Wild West Island is a Rattlesnake Wrangler costume that you can wear.

THE PLAINS INDIANS

Before Europeans settled the Great Plains, American Indians called this land home. The conflict between the native people and the settlers was far more complex—and terrible—than any childhood game of cowboys versus Indians.

Several American Indian tribes lived on the Great Plains before the West was settled by Europeans. They included the Blackfoot, Arapaho, Cree, Pawnee, and Cheyenne.

Ten thousand years ago: Native people were nomadic, traveling in small groups across the plains. They survived by gathering food and hunting.

1100: Settlements were formed as people practiced farming, which allowed them to stay in one place all year long. They fished and hunted animals, including bison and deer.

1750: By this year, the Spanish introduced horses to the plains, and the American Indians used them to make hunting easier. Before horses, hunters would work together to drive buffalo herds off the edge of a cliff. With horses, hunters could chase after the buffalo and keep pace with them.

1840s: As settlers blazed trails across the West, some tribes were angered by strangers trespassing on their land and attacked the pioneers.

1851: A temporary peace was brokered between tribes and the US government, giving tribes the legal right to their land.

1862: The Homestead Act brought more settlers to the plains, and tensions increased. Battles were waged between American Indians and the pioneers.

1876: That June, the government sent troops to remove Indians from their land in the Dakota Territory. A group of Sioux and Cheyenne attacked the troops as they tried to approach the Little Bighorn River. The attack left more than two hundred US soldiers dead, and became known as the Battle of the Little Bighorn.

1880s: Realizing they couldn't win a military battle against the native tribes, the US government encouraged the slaughter of buffalo, the main food source of the Plains Indians. The buffalo were hunted until they were almost extinct. Rather than starve, most Plains Indians gave up their land and moved to government reservations.

POP SOCIAL STUDIES

Many films about the Wild West show the Plains Indians living in tepees—cone-shaped tents made by draping animal skins over poles. While Plains Indians did use tepees, for most of the year they lived in earth lodges. As big as sixty feet in diameter, an earth lodge was shaped like a dome and lined with packed-in dirt.

GOLD RUSH!

What could make eighty thousand people abandon their daily lives and head to California? Not palm trees, amusement parks, or movie stars. Back in 1849, that's about how many people flocked to San Francisco to search for gold.

The gold rush began in 1848, near a mill owned by a man named John Sutter. He was having a sawmill built on the Sacramento River to cut lumber for his fort. One of his carpenters, James Marshall, was working in the riverbed when he found several flakes that looked like gold. He and Sutter tested it, and discovered that it was real.

They tried to keep it a secret, but the news got out a few months later. Word spread quickly around the country, and then the world. Fortune seekers flocked to Sutter's Mill, and it was reported that as much as $50,000 worth of gold was being mined every day.

By 1849, gold fever was raging. That year, as many as eighty thousand people traveled to California in hopes of getting rich. They became known as *forty-niners*. Before the gold rush was over, more than two hundred fifty thousand miners had traveled to California, but it wasn't the gold-paved paradise they had expected. Most of them didn't get rich. The mining camps were dangerous

Loud, rowdy miners were known as *hounds*.

places to live. Underground mines polluted the rivers. Many forty-niners left when the gold was gone, but others remained and helped settle California.

How to Pan for Gold

In Wild West Island, you can search for gold if you get a gold pan. A gold pan is a special pan with a flat bottom and shallow sides. The forty-niners used pans like this to help them locate loose pieces of gold in the gravelly soil of riverbeds. It's a simple process, but it takes patience:

1. The hardest part: Find a place where there is supposed to be gold.
2. Use the pan to scoop up a bunch of soil until the pan is about three-quarters full.
3. Bring the pan to running water, such as a stream or a river. Submerge the pan underwater. Break up the soil with your hands.
4. Gold will be heavier than the rocks, mud, and gravel you pick up. Move the pan from side to side so that the lighter stuff floats away. Push off the stuff that isn't gold and let the water carry it away.
5. Keep repeating this until you have sorted through all the gravel. If you're lucky, there will be pieces of gold at the bottom of the pan when you're done.

When some fortune seekers reached San Francisco, they took one look at the dangerous, crowded mining camps and turned right around and went home!

The San Francisco 49ers football team got its name from the forty-niners who took part in the gold rush.

LIFE ON A CATTLE RANCH

One of the first places you'll visit in Wild West Island is Rusty's Ranch. It's nothing fancy—a barn, a windmill, and a big ole corral—but ranches like this were an important part of shaping the West. They employed cowboys to watch over big herds of cattle as they grazed the plains, or to drive cattle for hundreds of miles to places where they would be sold and slaughtered.

The Spanish brought cattle to Mexico in the 1500s. More than two hundred years later, cattle ranching came to the American West from Mexico. In 1749, José de Escandón, the governor of a state in Mexico called Nuevo León, established the first western ranch in what we now know as southern Texas. Three thousand settlers and 146 soldiers started the ranch along the Rio Grande. As ranches spread across Texas, they sprung up next to water sources such as rivers or springs to service the thirsty cattle herds.

POP HISTORY

RUSTY'S RANCH

SO YOU WANT TO BE A COWBOY

Little kids pretend to be them. Hollywood loves to make movies about them. It's fun to dream about riding the open plains on a beautiful horse as the sun sets behind you. But in reality, the life of a cowboy was (and still is) filled with lots of hard work.

1870
HELP WANTED: COWBOY

Like working in the great outdoors? Then this is the job for you. You'll be driving a herd of two thousand cattle hundreds of miles from our ranch in Texas to Missouri, where they will be loaded onto trains and shipped northeast. The journey will take weeks, and you'll spend each day riding in the hot sun and each night sleeping under the stars. Sure, there might be a few dangerous thunderstorms and deadly rattlesnakes, but then it wouldn't be the great outdoors without them, would it?

You must also be able to defend yourself. Along the way, the herd will trample on land where they don't belong, making farmers and American Indians angry. And of course you've got to expect a few rustlers who will try to steal the cattle—and don't care if they kill you in the process.

So what are you waiting for? Come on down to the ranch and sign up for the big drive. It pays forty dollars a month! Coffee boilers need not apply.

Forty dollars in 1870 is more than $1,000 today.

Spanish Roots

The job of cowboy originated on the cattle ranches of Spain. They were called *vaqueros*, which is the Spanish word for cowboys. (In Spanish, *vaca* means cow.)

A *rustler* is a thief who steals livestock.

A *coffee boiler* is a lazy cowhand who would rather sit around the coffeepot than work.

POP STATS

On cattle drives, about 25 percent of the cowboys were freed African American slaves, as many as 15 percent were Mexican, and about two-thirds of them were in their teens or early twenties.

COWBOY GEAR

The life of a cowboy may have been hard, but at least the job came with some awesome swag!

From the Ranch to the Runway

Cowboy boots weren't made for walking—they're for horseback riding, since cowboys spent most of the time on their horses. The pointy toes were designed to slip into the stirrups, and the high heels prevented the shoes from slipping all the way through. If that happened, the cowboy's foot could get caught, and that could mean falling off the saddle and getting dragged by a running horse. Today, many people who have never been near a horse wear cowboy boots purely for fashion.

Spurs That Jingle Jangle Jingle

No, that isn't a pizza cutter on the heel of the boot—it's a spur, a metal wheel with spiked edges. A cowboy digs the spurs into the flanks of his horse to signal the horse to move faster. Each spur is attached to the ankle with a leather strap. Some cowboys add small metal weights called jingle bobs that make noise when the cowboy walks.

Can It Really Fit Ten Gallons?

With its wide brim and tall crown, the ten-gallon hat is

Cowboys sometimes called spurs can openers.

No, They're Not Leggings . . .

They're chaps, pieces of leather that are wrapped around the thighs and legs of the cowboy to protect him from the thorny brush on the plains.

the most notable part of any cowboy outfit. People sometimes think the hat was named because it could hold ten gallons of water—or looked like it could, anyway. But the name might have one of these origins:

The cowboy hat was originally designed in 1865 by John Stetson. The hat was nicknamed the "Boss of the Plains" and it is still manufactured today.

- In Spanish, *tan galán* means "so gallant,"

  The wide brim of the hat protected the cowboy from the sun and rain.

  and referred to the hats worn by the vaqueros, which were considered nicer than the sombreros worn by farmers. In English, the words sound like "ten gallon."
- *Galón* is the Spanish word for braid, and vaqueros used to wrap braids around the brim of their hats. So a hat with ten braids would be a *ten galón* hat.

More Than Just a Rope

Every cowboy carried a rawhide rope, also called a lariat, about fifty feet long and three-quarters of an inch thick. To corral an animal, a cowboy would make a lasso out of the rope by tying a noose in it—a loop with a knot that slides up and down the rope. The cowboy would throw the loop over the animal's head, and then pull on the long end of the rope to tighten the noose.

Bandanna

People today like to wear them as headbands, but a cowboy used them to cover his mouth, so he wouldn't eat a handful of dirt every time dust kicked up from the trail. It also protected his face from the sun and the cold.

A COWBOY'S BEST FRIEND

Without a horse, a cowboy just can't be a cowboy. It's like being a race-car driver without a car. The cowboy's horse would take him for miles across the plains on long cattle drives. During the height of the cowboy era, from the 1860s through the 1880s, you might have seen cowboys riding one of these horses:

Mule

A mule is the offspring of a female horse and a male donkey. They're smaller than horses, and it might be hard to picture a cowboy riding on one. But a mule proved to be an excellent choice for a cowboy. They're fast—they can actually run faster than some horses. They can go longer without food or water than horses, and they live longer, too.

Mustang

When you hear the word *mustang*, you might think of a horse that is wild, fast, and free. These horses do live in the wild, but they're technically not wild. That's because they are the descendants of horses brought by Spanish explorers, starting with Columbus. Some of these horses escaped, and by 1900, as many as two million mustangs were roaming free across the plains. The mustangs in the Wild West were most likely descended from a breed of horse called the Spanish Barb, a strong horse known for its intelligence and good temperament.

The word mustang comes from the Spanish word mesteño, which means "stray."

Appaloosa

On Wild West Island, you'll be asked to tame a horse named Elmer. He's most likely an Appaloosa. How can you tell? Like Elmer, Appaloosas have a spotted pattern on their coats. Spotted horses can be seen in the famous ancient cave paintings in France. Spanish explorers brought these horses to North America, where they were embraced by native tribes such as the Nez Perce. They bred them with other breeds to get a horse with amazing speed, agility, and a gentle disposition. The result is what we now call the American Appaloosa.

Saddlebreds and Thoroughbreds

Today, you might see distinguished Saddlebred horses competing in a horse show, and speedy Thoroughbreds competing on the racetrack. In the 1800s, these breeds were used by soldiers in the Civil War. When the war ended, some soldiers brought their horses with them to the cattle ranches of the West.

GIT ALONG, LITTLE DOGIES

Without herds of cattle to corral, there wouldn't have been much for a cowboy to do. Early in the nineteenth century, cattle in the Southwest were mainly used for their skin, which was made into leather, and their fat, which was made into candles and soap. But when northerners developed a taste for beef in the middle of the century, western ranchers could get rich by driving the cattle to railroad stations where they would be shipped out and sold for food.

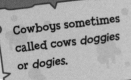

Cowboys sometimes called cows *doggies* or *dogies*.

Texas Longhorn

With its distinctive curved horns, this cattle breed is what most people think of when they think of the Old West. These hardy cows have long legs and hard hooves that come in handy when walking on miles of trails.

Longhorns weren't bred by humans to be perfect trail animals—they evolved naturally as descendants of Spanish cattle bred with other European cattle. These cattle almost went extinct after the decline of the cattle-ranching industry in the late nineteenth century. In the 1920s, the US government created a refuge for them, and today the breed is becoming more popular again with ranchers.

The longest horns on record for a Longhorn were more than eight feet wide from tip to tip!

American Brahman

Not all cattle in the Old West were sold for beef. The American Brahman is a dairy cow related to the Brahman cow of India. They were bred to tolerate the heat and are more resistant to insects and disease than some other breeds.

Angus

You've probably seen one of the many restaurant commercials out there bragging about the quality of their Angus beef. Those juicy steaks and burgers come from Angus cows, which were brought to the United States from Scotland in 1873. They are known for their black hair.

All cattle today are probably descended from the aurochs, a wild ox from Europe that has been extinct since 1627.

POP HISTORY

RIDING THE CHISHOLM TRAIL

In 1867, a cattle-shipping depot opened at the Kansas Pacific Railroad in Abilene, Kansas. Until 1871, cowboys drove cattle north from San Antonio, Texas, about one thousand miles to the depot. The trail taken was named the Chisholm Trail, probably after a trader named Jesse Chisholm.

About 1.5 million cattle were driven on the Chisholm Trail. The trail declined after depots opened in other cities. By the 1880s, the railroads had built branches all over the West, making long cattle drives unnecessary.

This trail line is more of a suggestion—the drive took a meandering path, depending on where the grass was growing, and factors like which areas were safest to pass through.

There was no official starting point for the trail. The drive began wherever the herd could be rounded up.

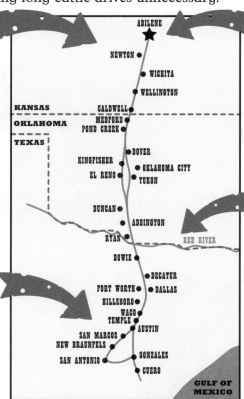

Abilene was a sleepy prairie village before it became a booming cow town filled with cowboys, merchants, and hard cases.

Crossing rivers could be a harrowing experience. Many cowboys died when rivers flooded or the current was too fast.

Watching Their Weight

Cattle could be driven as much as twenty-five miles per day, but at that pace they would lose too much weight before they got to market. So cowboys aimed for a slower pace of fifteen miles per day, which meant that getting from San Antonio to Abilene could take as long as two months.

Waddy You Say?

Many cowboys were young men—some as young as eleven or twelve years old. The younger cowboys were called *waddies*, and they were given the least exciting jobs on the trail, riding alongside and behind the herd.

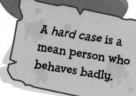

A hard case is a mean person who behaves badly.

TWENTY-FOUR HOURS ON THE CHISHOLM TRAIL

3:00 a.m.: The first person to wake up at camp is the cook. He'd start out by grinding the coffee that he'd brew in a pot of boiling water. There were no instant coffeemakers on the trail.

The camp cook would usually be nicknamed "cookie." Besides the trail boss, he was the second-highest paid worker (earning as much as seventy-five dollars a month), even though he didn't do any cattle herding. A cook had a lot of responsibilities, including taking care of sick cowboys and helping them write letters back home.

4:00 a.m.: The first cowboys to eat breakfast would be the ones getting ready to take over for the guys on night guard. The other cowboys would be up before sunrise to eat breakfast, start breaking up camp, and maybe washing off the trail dust in a nearby stream.

6:00 a.m.: Before sunup, all riders would saddle up to begin another long day on the trail. The trail boss would take the lead alongside the cook, who would carry all the camp supplies in a chuck wagon pulled by horses, or sometimes oxen.

10:00 a.m.: River crossing! Cows could easily get spooked in the rushing river water and drown. Cowboys would have to work hard to make sure the cattle stayed calm and didn't try to turn around in the water.

11:00 a.m.: In the middle of the day, the drive would come to a stop to give the cattle a rest, and let the cows in the back catch up to the herd.

Noon: Lunchtime—featuring more coffee to keep cowboys going during the day. They might use this break to give the horse they rode on a rest and saddle up a fresh horse.

1:00 p.m.: The drive kicks back into gear.

3:00 p.m.: Danger! A horse thief hidden in the hills takes a shot at the wrangler—and, thankfully, misses. The trail boss chases him away, but the wrangler has to scramble to herd the frightened horses.

8:00 p.m.: After fourteen hours on the trail, the long day is finally over. Time for cowboys to eat another meal prepared by the cook (with more coffee, of course) and then spread out their bedrolls under the stars. If they were lucky, bedbugs, mosquitoes, scorpions, or snakes wouldn't bite them during the night. If you were on night guard duty, you wouldn't be able to get any shut-eye for the next two or four hours, depending on the length of your shift.

JOBS ON THE TRAIL

Trail Boss: the guy in charge

Cook: also barber, banker, dentist, doctor, and advice giver

Point Man: one of two experienced cowboys who steer the herd

Swing: a strong rider who rides behind the point man

Flank: less experienced cowboys who ride alongside the herd and keep the cows from straying away

Drag Rider: The job usually reserved for newbies. They ride behind the herd and swallow most of the dust kicked up by the cattle.

Wrangler: an inexperienced cowboy in charge of the extra horses on the drive

COWBOY GRUB

You might not have time to chow down while you're racing around Wild West Island, but cowboys looked forward to three hearty meals a day.

Breakfast

Coffee: Coffee beans weren't always easy to get, so substitutes were often used—such as acorns or roasted peas.

Biscuits: Fluffy biscuits were cooked in a dutch oven and were good for sopping up gravy or filling with beans.

Cornmeal mush

Pancakes or johnnycakes (pancakes made from cornmeal)

Bacon (if you were lucky)

Dried fruit

Lunch

Coffee

Roast beef or fried beef

Beans: Mexican red beans were cheap and easy to transport, but they took a long time to cook. At the end of the day, the cook might travel ahead of the others to get the beans started early.

Biscuits

Another nickname for a cook was a biscuit shooter.

Chuck is a word for cheap cuts of meat—like the kind that might be cooked up on a cattle drive.

Dinner

Coffee

Beef stew: There were no big, juicy steaks for these cowboys. Cooks were provided with tough cuts of meat that tasted best when chopped up and cooked for a long time with liquid, potatoes, and other vegetables.

Bread

Dessert: A nice cook might make a peach cobbler or apple pie, especially if fresh fruit could be found along the trail.

Meringue is a fluffy pie topping made from egg whites. Cowboys liked to call it calf slobber.

Before There Were RVs . . .

In the early days of trail riding, cowboys carried their food and supplies with them—usually some dried beef and rock-hard biscuits. Then, in 1866, a cattle rancher named Charles Goodnight had a bright idea. He took an old army wagon and tricked it out with a big pantry box with lots of shelves and drawers to hold supplies. The top could be used as a worktable. He added another box to hold the really big pans, and the first chuck wagon was born. Chuck wagons were used to hold all kinds of items, including bedrolls, first aid supplies, and blacksmithing tools.

CROSSING THE WILD FRONTIER

Not everyone who traveled across the Wild West was a cowboy. Pioneers came to the West to start farms, open businesses in new towns, or simply start a new life. They came on foot, by horse, by wagon, and eventually by train, and the trails they blazed helped shape the future of the United States.

THE WAY OUT WEST

One of the most important ways for travelers to get out west—way out west—was the Oregon Trail. Fur trappers and missionaries were some of the first to blaze the two-thousand-mile passage from Missouri to Oregon. They stayed close to the winding rivers so that they could always be near fresh water. Others followed, and between the 1840s and 1860s, an estimated four hundred thousand people took the trail west.

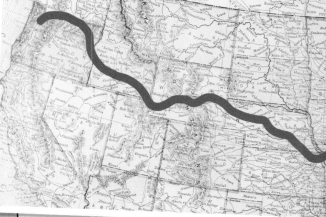

Take the Trail!

START
Your journey begins in Independence, Missouri, near the Kansas border. You're traveling in a wagon called a prairie schooner, pulled by mules. For most of the two-thousand-mile trip, you walk alongside because the wagon is crowded with supplies and the ride is bumpy.

Fort Kearny
You've made it to Nebraska. Here, you can buy new supplies and meet travelers coming from the East on other trails.

Chimney Rock
From the trail, you can see this 325-foot-tall needle-shaped rock—a natural landmark that lets you know you're about one-third of the way there.

Fort Laramie

You've reached a major supply stop on your journey—a military post that started out as an Indian trading post.

South Pass

This twenty-mile-wide valley that passes through the Rocky Mountains was an important landmark on the journey. Until it was discovered, traveling across the Rocky Mountains was difficult and dangerous.

Fast Food

Hankering for some fresh meat? Go hunting! Be on the lookout for animals such as bison, antelope, jackrabbits, deer, and ducks. And don't forget the rivers and streams, which are loaded with fish.

Fort Bridger

Stock up on supplies again—and say good-bye to any Mormon friends you may have met, who will be taking a different route from here into Utah.

Three Island Crossing

How's your luck? If the water in the Snake River is low enough, you can cross it and take the northern branch of the river, which is an easier route. If not, you've got to stay south.

Flagstaff

See those blue mountain peaks in the distance? They're the Blue Mountains, a sign that you've almost reached the end of the trail.

END

It's been four months since you left Missouri, and you've reached Oregon City—the end of the trail. You can stay and settle here, or cross the Columbia River and see what's happening at busy Fort Vancouver.

The Dalles

Now you're faced with a tough choice. You can take apart your wagon, put it on a boat, and sail down the rough waters of the Columbia River. Or (if it's after 1846), you can make a steep climb to the Barlow Pass and stay on land. Both routes will take you to Oregon City.

If you wanted to travel from Missouri to Oregon today, it would take about six and a half hours by plane, and cost about four hundred dollars.

THAT'S A REALLY BIG BUTTE!

If you visit Wild West Island, you'll explore the town of Dusty Gulch, ride the Diamond Plains, and battle bandits in Rock Ridge. All these places are named after the geographical features you'd find in the West. Don't know a gulch from a gully? Then check out these pages and you'll be able to navigate the Wild West like a seasoned cowhand.

- **Butte**: An isolated hill with steep sides; there are no other hills or mountains around it. The word is pronounced "byoot," as in, "That hill is a real butte!"
- **Canyon**: A wide, deep opening between hills with very steep sides, usually with a river running through it
- **Cave**: A large hole in the side of a hill or a cliff, or under the ground

- **Cliff**: The steep face of a large rock or mountain
- **Desert**: A dry area of land, usually covered with sand, and without a lot of plants growing on it
- **Gorge**: A narrow opening between hills with steep, rocky sides. There is usually a stream running through it.
- **Gulch**: A deep, narrow opening between hills, usually one with water running through it

- **Gully**: Like a gulch, but smaller. Usually it's been worn away by running water, and when it rains, excess water pours through it.
- **Mesa**: A hill with a flat top and steep sides, with no other hills around it

- **Plain**: A large area of mostly flat land
- **Ravine**: A narrow opening between hills that was formed by running water. A ravine has steep sides and is larger than a gully but smaller than a canyon.
- **Ridge**: A long, narrow mountain range
- **Valley**: A low area of land between hills or mountains. Many valleys were formed millions of years ago by glaciers that carved them out of the land.

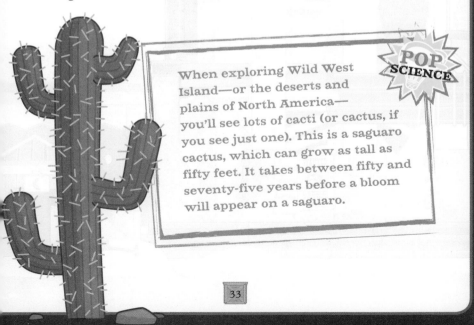

POP SCIENCE

When exploring Wild West Island—or the deserts and plains of North America—you'll see lots of cacti (or cactus, if you see just one). This is a saguaro cactus, which can grow as tall as fifty feet. It takes between fifty and seventy-five years before a bloom will appear on a saguaro.

THE PONY EXPRESS

When you get to the town of Dusty Gulch on Wild West Island, you'll be greeted by an exhausted Pony Express rider who needs your help to deliver the mail to the next town. When you help her out, you're taking part in history.

Before the Pony Express started on April 3, 1860, there was no way to get a message across the West quickly. Forget about cell phones—there were no telegraphs or telephone lines, only stagecoaches making their way across the miles, or steamships that had to travel around South America to get from the East Coast to the West Coast.

The Pony Express changed that. It was a bold idea—get riders to carry small packages on horseback two thousand miles from Missouri to California, handing off the packages to fresh riders along the route. Riding at top speed, they could make the trip in ten days.

FIRST
Historians can't agree, but the first rider was either a guy named Johnny Fry or Billie Richardson.

DISTANCE
During the eighteen months that the Pony Express was in business, riders traveled about 650,000 miles on horseback.

STOPS
Historians estimate that there were 190 stops along the route.

COST
Sending a letter was expensive—five dollars for a package weighing half an ounce. That's the equivalent of ninety-five dollars today.

DANGERS
According to folklore, one rider was killed by American Indians, and one bag of mail was lost on the express.

LEGEND
"Pony Bob" Haslam was twenty years old when he made the longest round-trip ride on the express: 380 miles. His route took him through Paiute Indian territory at a time when tensions were high, and his relief rider refused to take his place.

SPEED
The ten-day record was broken by riders delivering the text of President Lincoln's inaugural address. It reached California in fewer than eight days. (One of the riders on this trip was Pony Bob, who rode 120 miles while wounded, making him a Pony Express legend.)

THE END
The Pony Express came to a halt in October 1861, when the first transcontinental telegraph allowed people to send messages over wires more quickly and easily.

THE TRANSCONTINENTAL RAIL LINE

It was definitely the greatest building project of the nineteenth century. It also changed the face of America more than any other event that century, except the Civil War.

1814
British engineer George Stephenson builds the first steam locomotive engine that can run on rails.

1825
In England, Stephenson builds the first passenger steam railway in the world.

1828
Construction begins on the first passenger railway in the United States—the Baltimore and Ohio Railroad.

1862
Congress passes the first Pacific Railway Act. This gave the Central Pacific Railroad Company the right to build a railroad heading east from California. It also gave the Union Pacific Railroad Company the right to build a railway heading west from Nebraska. The idea was that when these two lines met, there would be one long railway traveling across the West.

1863
The Central Pacific starts laying track heading east from California.

1869
The two lines meet in Promontory Summit, Utah, and a golden railroad spike is driven to mark the occasion. Workers have laid 1,800 miles of track.

1865
The Union Pacific starts laying track heading west from Nebraska with a crew of Irish immigrants and Civil War veterans. These workers also faced illnesses from tainted water (the Chinese boiled theirs to make tea) and from poor hygiene. (Unlike the Chinese, they did not believe in bathing.)

1865
To meet the demand for workers, the Central Pacific hires thousands of Chinese laborers. They earned twenty-eight dollars a month (less than other workers) and faced dangers as they blasted explosives through solid rock to make tunnels.

BANDIT MAGNETS

As you ride the train in Wild West Island, you'll be attacked by the Grande Gang on horseback. Train robberies became common as bad guys realized that the trains could carry large quantities of valuable goods.

The first robbery of a moving train in the United States took place on October 6, 1866. A gang called the Reno brothers figured that if they stopped a train in the middle of nowhere, they could get away without the law coming after them. They were right. They stopped a train in Indiana, took $14,000 at gunpoint, and made a clean getaway.

Other gangs copied this idea, and train robberies were a big problem until the railroad companies figured out some solutions. They stored valuables in huge safes that were too heavy to carry away. The Union Pacific line started posting guards and horses on trains so they could give chase if necessary. By the end of the nineteenth century, train robbing wasn't such a popular pastime for bad guys anymore.

TRADING POSTS

The town of Dusty Gulch on Wild West Island wouldn't be complete without a trading post. Neither would any town in the real Wild West. Think about it. If you needed a new jacket or cooking pot, you might be able to order one from the East, but you might have to wait months for a stagecoach to deliver it (especially before the rail lines were in business). But if you lived near a trading post, just about everything you needed could be found in one place.

Trading posts in North America began in the fifteenth century, when American Indians traded furs to European explorers and settlers. At the time, coins weren't of any use to the Indians, so they exchanged the furs for items such as

UP FOR A TRADE?

Here are just a few of the items you could get at a trading post:

- Fur (beaver was popular because it was waterproof)
- Guns
- Cooking tools
- Fabric, thread, and needles
- Hats and shoes
- Candles
- Tea, salt, sugar, and spices
- Jewelry

food or tools. The furs were taken to Europe, and a huge demand grew.

As the fur trade boomed, trading posts sprouted up. Merchants built log cabins to store their goods for sale. Soon, the trading posts became destination points—word got around that you could sell and get goods there. As the country grew, some of the posts expanded and became forts where soldiers were stationed. Towns sprouted up around trading posts. The West couldn't have grown without them.

If you *dickered* over a trade, it meant that you were trying to negotiate with the trader for a better deal.

Gold Pan

LIFE IN A WILD WEST TOWN

You'll meet lots of interesting characters in Dusty Gulch—some want to trade with you, some want to trick you, some want to help you, and some want you to help them.

A typical town in the real Wild West would have a lot of interesting characters, too. After all, it wasn't easy to move to the frontier and start a new life. Some came to make their fortunes, and others came to try something new, but they all had one thing in common: a spirit of adventure. And when all those exciting people got together in one place, you can be sure that it resulted in some memorable stories.

MEET ME AT THE SALOON

Where did you go in the Old West if you were hungry, thirsty, or itching for some entertainment? To the local saloon! The saloon was the main gathering place for cowhands, merchants, ranchers, miners, and weary travelers.

NO GIRLS ALLOWED

The only women allowed in the saloon were the ones who worked there.

WE NEVER CLOSE

Many saloons stayed open twenty-four hours, seven days a week.

LIVE MUSIC!

Imagine living with no radios, smartphones, televisions, or movie theaters. People on the frontier were desperate for entertainment. One story says that an Irish fiddler who worked in an Idaho City saloon had a special platform built underneath him. If a gunfight started in the saloon, pulleys lifted the platform so he could keep playing without getting shot.

PRIZEFIGHT TONIGHT!

Amateur boxing matches were popular attractions at saloons. You didn't need any fancy equipment—just a lot of room and two willing men.

BAD BEHAVIOR

You can only get root beer at Ruby's saloon, but in a Wild West saloon, patrons came to drink alcohol—and lots of it. This often led to arguments and violent brawls.

CARD PLAYING ALLOWED

Friendly (and not-so-friendly) games were a popular way to pass the time. In Ruby's Root Beer Saloon, you'll face two men in a gum-chewing contest called Spit-n-Time.

COME SEE OUR NEW STAGE!

Some enterprising saloon owners built stages, and theater companies from the East traveled west to perform full-blown plays.

MEETING TONIGHT

Because a saloon was usually the largest building in town, it was the place where meetings were held before town halls were built.

PHOTOGRAPHY STAND

As soon as people started heading out west, those back home in the North and East were very curious. What did it look like out there?

So, the government teams sent to explore the West usually had a photographer with them. Most used a device called a box camera. A photo could be taken in a few simple steps:

1. The camera would go on a tripod to ensure the image would be steady and not blurry.

2. The photographer would coat a glass plate with collodion, a highly flammable chemical.

3. The plate would be inserted into the camera.

4. After taking the photo, the photographer would have to quickly take the glass plate into a darkroom, usually a wagon or even a tent, to develop the photo on paper.

One of the most famous traveling photographers in the Old West was Timothy O'Sullivan. After photographing Civil War battlefields, he joined a government team as a photographer. He traveled around the West in the 1860s and 1870s, shooting breathtaking photos of the landscape, pioneers, and American Indians.

POP HISTORY

TRAVELING CON MEN

In Rock Ridge, you'll see a colorful wagon advertising "R.J. Earl's Genuine Elixirs, Fixers, and Magnificent Mixers." If you can pay him, he'll sell you one of his amazing concoctions that can turn you invisible, make your head huge, or give you other impossible powers.

In the real Wild West, there were plenty of men like R.J. Earl, trying to sell potions that promised cures and powers to those who bought them. But unlike R.J. Earl, their products didn't work. They were called snake oil salesmen, or quacks.

Snake Oil Salesman

This term has its roots with the Chinese laborers who built the railroad. They brought their traditional medicine practices with them, and used the oil from a sea snake to treat arthritis.

When word got around that this cure worked, non-Chinese people decided to make their own snake oil remedies, but without the benefit of Chinese tradition. They claimed to make it from rattlesnake oil, although many spared themselves the trouble of hunting rattlesnakes and made theirs from beef fat. Neither formula lived up to its claims, and soon any medicine that didn't deliver what it promised was called snake oil.

Quack

Before the snake oil craze, someone selling impossible cures was called a quack. The term may have come from the Dutch word *quacksalver,* meaning "a boaster who applies salve" (as in a medicinal salve). It also might come from the German word *quacksalber,* which means "questionable salesperson."

A WILD TIME IN DODGE CITY

Ask anyone to name a town from the Wild West, and they'll probably say, "Dodge City." So why is this Kansas town so legendary?

Great Location: Dodge City was at the start of the Santa Fe Trail, which led from Franklin, Missouri, to Santa Fe, New Mexico. Thousands of pioneers used this trail to take them west. In 1872, three railroad lines stopped at the city.

Safety: Fort Dodge was right next to the city, offering a safe place to stay during conflicts with American Indians. Mail was also delivered to the fort—another plus.

Buffalo Country: Hunters flocked to Dodge City to

hunt the enormous herds of buffalo. They left the meat and shipped the buffalo hide and bone back home. This boom lasted until the buffalo, sadly, were hunted to near extinction.

Cattle Depot: The Chisholm Trail (see page 22) eventually branched off, and more than five million cattle were driven into Dodge City during the height of the long-distance cattle drives.

Famous Lawmen: As Dodge City got busier and busier, lawmen such as Wyatt Earp and Bat Masterson came into town to help keep the peace.

Plenty of Saloons: In 1887, Dodge City had one thousand residents—and seventeen saloons.

RUNNER-UP: TOMBSTONE

This silver-mining town lies in southeast Arizona. It is most famous for being the site of the battle at the OK Corral, a gunfight between lawmen and a gang of outlaw cowboys.

Surprisingly, the town didn't get its name from the battles and feuds fought there. Some say it was named by the town's founder, Ed Schieffelin, who was told he would only find his tombstone there, but found silver instead. Or it might have been named for nearby granite rocks that looked like tombstones.

If you ever hear someone say, "Let's get out of Dodge," it means they want to leave wherever they are before trouble starts.

POP ENGLISH

LAWMEN VERSUS OUTLAWS

In the early days of the West, there were plenty of opportunities for honest men to make money—and for bad guys to steal it from them. As towns started springing up far from big cities, there were no police departments to keep crime at bay.

When you get to Diamond Plains, the marshal there will give you his badge so you can get past the Grande Gang. In real life, a US Marshal could choose his own deputy and pass on his badge. (They can't do that anymore.)

Some towns might hire a sheriff—if they could find anyone brave enough to take the job. But for many people in the West, their only protection came from the US Marshals. In 1789, George Washington appointed the first thirteen marshals, and Congress gave them the power to enforce laws in any part of the nation. They were sent west to maintain law and order where there was none, and to try to keep peace with the settlers and the American Indians.

MEET THE BAD GUYS

These villains are some of the most notorious criminals to darken the plains of the wild frontier. All of them ended up in the calaboose—or as cold as a wagon tire.

JESSE JAMES and FRANK JAMES

Jesse: 1847-1882
Frank: 1843-1915

Calaboose is slang for jail. Someone "as cold as a wagon tire" is dead.

Sons of a Baptist minister, Jesse and Frank grew up on their family's farm in Missouri. They both fought with the South in the Civil War. When the conflict ended, they started robbing banks, trains, and other businesses that were owned or operated by the North. Jesse and Frank formed the James gang, committing more than twenty robberies and an untold number of murders.

Jesse and Frank may have robbed together, but they didn't die together. Jesse died in 1882, at the hands of one of his own gang members, Robert Ford. There was a $10,000 reward for the brothers, dead or alive, and Ford shot Jesse and claimed the money. Frank went to trial, but wasn't convicted. He lived out the rest of his days on the right side of the law.

A bounty jumper was someone who took money to join the army, and then ran off without serving his duty.

BILLY THE KID

WANTED

Dead or Alive

1859 or 1860–1881

Billy the Kid was born William H. Bonney (or maybe Henry McCarty—historians aren't sure) in New York City. He was nicknamed "the Kid" because he was a teenager when he committed most of his crimes—including the murders of as many as twenty-seven men.

Billy's troubles started after he left New York with his parents. They settled in Kansas, but his father died when Billy was a child. Billy's mother moved to Colorado, remarried, and then the family moved to New Mexico. When he was fifteen, his mother died, and Billy started hanging around with the Southwest gangs and getting into trouble. After being found guilty of murder in 1881, Billy escaped jail. But Sheriff Patrick Floyd Garrett tracked him down, and that was the end of Billy the Kid.

THE RENO BROTHERS GANG

Frank: 1837–1868
John: 1838–1895
Simeon: 1843–1868
William: 1848–1868

Burglary, bribery, horse theft, arson, bounty jumping, train robbing, treasury robbing, murder—it's almost easier to list the crimes the Reno brothers didn't commit than the ones they did. There were other members of the gang, but the four Reno brothers were at the core— Frank, John, Simeon, and William.

Growing up on a farm in a strict religious family, the Reno brothers rebelled and began terrorizing the Midwest as soon as they were old enough. The gang's most famous crime was their robbery of a moving train on October 6, 1866. They were the first outlaws ever to try it, and they succeeded. But their success didn't last long. The famous Pinkerton Detective Agency targeted them, and by 1868, John was sentenced to prison, and Frank, Simeon, and William were hanged for their crimes.

BELLE STARR

1848-1889

How do you go from being a model student at a girls' school to a Bandit Queen? It probably started when Belle (born Myra Belle Shirley) was a teenage volunteer during the Civil War. Belle helped the Confederacy by reporting the position of Union troops. After the war was over, many Confederate soldiers became outlaws, and Belle's family gave them refuge at their farm.

Belle ended up marrying a fellow soldier-turned-outlaw named Jim Reed. She used the gold from one of his bank robberies to buy fancy clothes, and would ride through the streets shooting off pistols.

Jim Reed was killed by a deputy sheriff after a stagecoach robbery, and Belle married a Cherokee Indian named Sam Starr. Their ranch became an outlaw hideout, and Belle participated in horse thieving and the robbing of a post office. She was shot by an unknown assailant in 1889, and a book was published about her: *Belle Starr, the Bandit Queen, or the Female Jesse James.*

When she attended the Carthage Female Academy in her childhood, Belle did well in many subjects, including arithmetic, Greek, and Latin.

DOC HOLLIDAY

1852–1887

Was John Henry Holliday a good guy or a bad guy? A weak dentist or a hard-living gunman? The truth is in there somewhere. Born in Georgia, he was indeed a dentist, but he turned to gambling after he moved to Dallas, Texas, and discovered he was good at it. At the time, he knew he was dying a slow death from tuberculosis, and he wasn't a strong man. He started practicing with a six-shooter to protect himself during gambling disputes, and became known for his shooting skills. A hot temper and a six-gun led Doc into many gunfights, and he killed several men. While fleeing from the law, he met up with Wyatt Earp, and helped him during the fight at the OK Corral. The law never caught up to him—but his tuberculosis did. He died from the disease when he was thirty-five years old.

BUSTED!

WANTED

Wanted posters for criminals, like the one you'll see in Dusty Gulch, weren't common until around 1900, when techniques in photography improved. Before then, postcards were mailed to law officers with written descriptions of the lawbreakers.

MEET THE (SOMETIMES) GOOD GUYS

Just hearing the names of these lawmen could strike fear in the heart of the most dangerous villain.

WYATT EARP

1848-1929

Looking at Wyatt Earp's life is like reading a history of the Old West. He and his family trekked from the Midwest to California near the end of the Civil War. He worked on a crew for the Union Pacific Railroad; became an assistant marshal for Dodge City, Kansas; mined for gold in the Black Hills of South Dakota; and worked as a stagecoach guard for the Wells Fargo company.

In 1878, he ended up in Tombstone, Arizona, where his brother Virgil was marshal. He became a gambler, and when his family got into a feud with the Clanton gang, he participated in the famous gunfight at the OK Corral. That's about when Earp's good-guy status became fuzzy. Some thought that the fight against the Clantons was personal, and not about enforcing the law. Then, a year later, Wyatt's brother Morgan was shot dead. Wyatt and his brother Warren killed two of the suspects, and Wyatt lived the rest of his life with charges of murder hanging over his head.

WANTED

Dead or Aliv

WILD BILL HICKOK

1837–1876

Born James Butler Hickok in Illinois, Wild Bill is one of the West's biggest legends. Growing up, his family's home was a stop on the Underground Railroad. He joined the antislavery movement, and fought with the Union army. It was during the war that Wild Bill became a legend. He was staying at a friend's house when he single-handedly defeated ten gang members who burst into the cabin. At least, that's what *Harper's New Monthly Magazine* reported, and people ate up the story.

After serving as sheriff of Hays City, Kansas, he became marshal of the busy cattle town Abilene, Kansas, in 1871. Many credit him with bringing law and order to the Old West, but he did kill several men in gunfights. His dangerous life caught up to him in 1876, when he was shot and killed during a poker game in a saloon.

BAT MASTERSON

1853–1921

Like other western lawmen, Bat Masterson held many jobs in his life and had a checkered past. Over his lifetime, he worked as a buffalo hunter, Indian scout, saloon keeper, and sportswriter. And as for the checkered part: In 1876, he killed two people in Texas after an argument.

What ranks Bat Masterson as a legendary lawman are the days he spent as a sheriff in Kansas, and as a deputy US marshal in Dodge City. He also became friends with Wyatt Earp in Tombstone. Bat Masterson wore a marshal's badge again when he later served as a deputy US marshal in New York.

Bat Masterson was born in Canada, but spent his childhood on farms in New York and the Midwest.

BAT MASTERSON.

PATRICK FLOYD GARRETT

1850-1908

He was "the man who shot Billy the Kid." Some people thought he was a hero, but others thought him a villain for shooting Billy, who had become a folk hero even though he was a criminal. The story was even more complicated because Patrick and Billy were friends. A former cowboy, Patrick got his start in law by protecting herds from cattle rustlers. He went on to work as a bartender in a saloon in New Mexico, and that's where he met Billy. They became friends who gambled together.

Then, in 1880, Patrick was appointed county sheriff, and he made it his goal to apprehend his outlaw friend. It took several months to track down Billy the Kid, but Patrick was successful, and ended up shooting and killing him. As a result, he lost his next election for sheriff. He went on to write a book about Billy the Kid—but it didn't sell well (probably because the market was already flooded with books about Billy).

MEET THE SHARPSHOOTERS

Besides breaking or enforcing the law, another way to get famous in the Wild West was to develop impressive shooting skills. In Wild West Island, you can test your skills at a shooting contest in the town of Dos Cactos. One of the opponents you'll face is Annie Oakley—one of the most bang-up sharpshooters ever to hold a pistol.

ANNIE OAKLEY

1860–1926

She was Phoebe Ann Mosey when she was born, became Annie Oakley when she started performing as a markswoman, and has gone down in history as "Little Sure Shot." So how did a girl from Ohio become such a famous shooter?

The stories say she came to it naturally, hunting animals when she was just a kid—enough to pay off the mortgage on her family's farm. When she was fifteen, she got into a shooting contest against a vaudeville performer named Frank Butler. Annie won the contest, married Butler, changed her name, and started performing with her husband onstage and in circuses.

Her real fame arrived when she joined Buffalo Bill Cody's Wild West show. She amazed audiences with her stunts: shooting dimes tossed in the air, or shooting so many bullets into an airborne playing card that it would end up looking like Swiss cheese. Before her career ended, she had performed for people all over the world—including Queen Victoria.

BUFFALO BILL CODY

1846-1917

Like many of these western legends, William F. Cody's life reads like an exciting novel. He started out as a cowboy when he was eleven years old. On one cattle drive, Wild Bill Hickok saved William during a fight with another man. At fourteen, historians think he rode for the Pony Express. He served the Union in the Civil War and hunted buffalo on the Great Plains.

Stories about "Buffalo Bill" Cody started appearing in newspapers and books, and he took advantage of that fame to start his Wild West show. He created an amazing spectacle with hundreds of performers who would reenact buffalo hunts, stagecoach robberies, and sharpshooting demonstrations. The show played to millions. He kept performing up until two months before his death at age seventy.

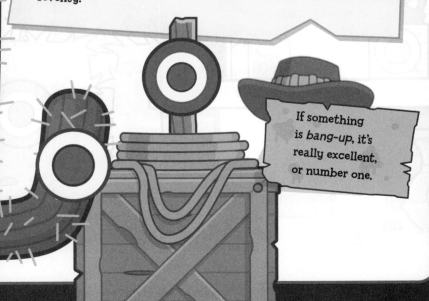

If something is *bang-up*, it's really excellent, or number one.

POP QUIZ

1. WHICH WILD WEST JOB WOULD YOU HAVE BEEN BEST AT?

A. COWHAND

B. GOLD MINER

C. SALOON KEEPER

2. HAVE YOU EVER RIDDEN A HORSE?

A. ALL THE TIME

B. NO

C. YES, AND I LOVED IT

D. YES, AND I'LL NEVER DO IT AGAIN

3. WHICH WILD WEST LEGEND WOULD YOU MEET IF YOU COULD?

A. BILLY THE KID

B. WYATT EARP

C. ANNIE OAKLEY

4. WHICH JOB DO YOU THINK IS MORE DANGEROUS?

A. TAMING A WILD HORSE

B. LEADING A CATTLE DRIVE

C. BUILDING THE CENTRAL PACIFIC RAILROAD

5. WHICH WILD WEST SKILL WOULD YOU MOST LIKE TO LEARN?

A. PANNING FOR GOLD

B. SHARPSHOOTING

C. COOKING OVER AN OPEN FIRE

D. HORSEBACK RIDING

6. IF YOU HAD TO RIDE A HORSE, WOULD YOU RATHER RIDE . . .

A. . . . A MULE?

B. . . . A MUSTANG?

C. . . . AN APPALOOSA?

7. HAVE YOU EVER TRAVELED WEST OF THE ROCKY MOUNTAINS?

A. YES

B. NO

C. UM, I LIVE THERE!

8. IF YOU HAD TO WEAR ONE ITEM OF COWBOY GEAR TO SCHOOL EVERY DAY, WOULD IT BE . . .

A. . . . BOOTS?

B. . . . A TEN-GALLON HAT?

C. . . . A BANDANNA?

9. HAVE YOU EVER SLEPT OUTSIDE UNDER THE STARS?

A. YES

B. NO

C. YES, AND I NEVER WILL AGAIN

10. WHICH COWBOY DISH WOULD YOU MOST LIKE TO EAT?

A. BEEF STEW

B. BISCUITS AND BEANS

C. PEACH PIE

Index